The Horses the Indians Rode

The Horses the Indians Rode

SIGMUND A. LAVINE

Illustrated with photographs and old prints

DODD, MEAD & COMPANY · NEW YORK

Frontispiece: *Cyrus Dallin's "The Appeal to the Great Spirit" is considered one of the most notable of American sculptures.* COURTESY, MUSEUM OF FINE ARTS, BOSTON, GIFT OF PETER C. BROOKS AND OTHERS

ISBN: 0-396-06980-0

Library of Congress Catalog Card Number: 74-3778

Printed in the United States of America

Illustrations courtesy of:

American Quarter Horse Association, 55 *top; Appaloosa News*, 71 *bottom*; Sterling and Francine Clark Art Institute, Williamstown, Massachusetts, 39; Maura and Thomas Haytman, 69, 70, 71 *top*, 73; International Arabian Horse Association, 66, 67; Ailleen Jensen, 38, after an old painting; Museum of Fine Arts, Boston, Gift of Peter C. Brooks and others, *frontispiece*; Museum of Fine Arts, Boston, M. and M. Karolik Collection, 30, 40 *top*; New York Racing Association—Paul Schafer, 55 *bottom*; St. Francis Mission, The Rosebud Educational Society, St. Francis, South Dakota, 51, 65; Sante Fe Railway Photos, 74, 75; Sam Savitt, 23; Smithsonian Institution National Anthropological Archives, Bureau of American Ethnological Collection, 17 *bottom*, 19, 26, 27, 28, 31, 32, 33, 34, 35, 36, 37, 41, 43, 44, 45, 46, 50, 52 *bottom*, 59, 61, 62, 63, 64; Toad Hill Stud Farm, Athol, New York, 48; Travelers Insurance Companies, 57, 60; Treasure Products, Inc., publisher of the C.M. Russell *Boyhood Sketchbook*, Bozeman, Montana, 40 *bottom*; United States Department of the Interior, Bureau of Land Management, 8, 25, 56, 58, 76; United States Department of the Interior, National Park Service, Photograph by Cecil W. Stoughton, 21.

For Leo—

who enjoys stories of the past even as he seeks scientific ways to shape the future

Contents

The Indians of Guatemala thought Cortez' black stallion, El Morzillo, was a god so they fashioned an idol of it in stone.

1

"Everything must have a beginning."

"Run for your lives! Our only hope is to reach the boat," shouted Friar Juan de Orbita.

As the Indians pelted them with stones, the band of Franciscans, bleeding and bruised, dashed down the path that led to the water's edge and tumbled into their craft. Casting off, they made their escape as the stones splashed on all sides.

This was not the first time Father Orbita and his fellow missionaries had faced death in the lush jungles of Guatemala. However, past dangers had been forgotten when they reached an island in Lake Petén. Not only did the natives welcome the Franciscans warmly but also they held a feast in their honor. The padres were then taken to see the islanders' most prized possession—a stone idol representing a black horse.

To the amazement of the Indians, Orbita seized a stout club and smashed the horse to pieces. Amazement gave way to fury when the chief screamed, "Kill them! Kill them! They are destroying the great god Tzomin-Chac!" At once, the Indians began bombarding the Spaniards with stones.

If Orbita had controlled his religious zeal and asked why his hosts worshiped the image of a horse, he would have heard a strange tale. It begins in 1525, when Cortez led an expedition into Central America in search of glory and treasure. By the time the conqueror of Mexico reached the Petén district of northern Guatemala, his magnificent black stallion El Morzillo was exhausted. So Cortez left the animal with the local tribesmen and gave them strict orders to nurse it back to health. He would, he promised, return.

El Morzillo was the first horse the Indians had ever seen. Convinced that it was a four-legged god, they offered it the same sacrifices they presented to their tribal divinities—cooked meats and garlands of flowers. The horse soon died of starvation. Fearful of Cortez's wrath and sure that they had somehow offended a powerful deity, the Indians fashioned a stone statue of the black stallion and worshiped it.

No one knows if the islanders replaced the idol destroyed by Orbita. However, history does record that Martin de Ursua was stunned by the reaction of the people of Petén to his black stallion when he rode through that area in 1697. Crowds danced wildly around his mount, shrieking with joy. Eventually De Ursua learned why his charger caused so much excitement. A horse had not been seen in Petén for nearly 175 years and the Indians thought El Morzillo had come back to them.

The horses ridden by Cortez and De Ursua would not have excited the nomadic tribesmen who entered Alaska from Asia between twenty-five and fifty thousand years ago to become the ancestors of the Indians. At that time horses roamed throughout the New World and were among the most numerous of animals in both North and South America. The earliest red men did not consider the horse a god but a source of easily acquired food. Huge numbers of horse bones have been unearthed by archaeologists—students of man's past—at the buried campsites of these primitive hunters.

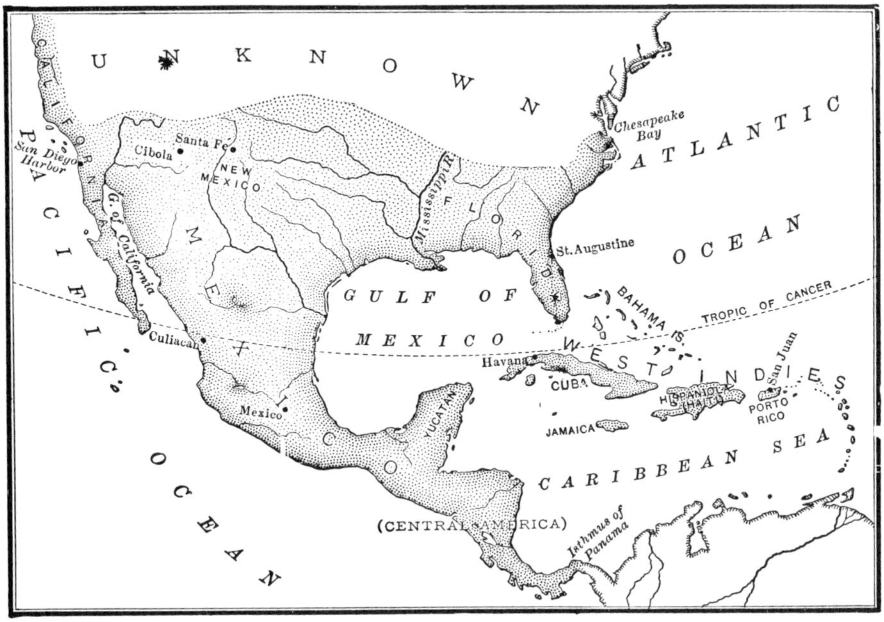

An old map of Spanish North America. Guatemala lies just below the Yucatan Peninsula.

Meanwhile, until a geological upheaval created the Bering Strait and destroyed the land bridge connecting the Eastern and Western Hemispheres, herds of horses migrated to the Old World. It was well that they did. Otherwise, the horse would have become extinct. By 900 B.C., horses had vanished from the Americas, the victims of a mysterious plague.

There is little doubt that for centuries tribal taletellers recounted stories of the tremendous horse herds that once galloped over the New World. But by the time "a certayne caravell . . . was driven to a lande unknowne, and not described on any Map or Carde of the Sea" and Columbus dropped anchor in the West Indies, the inhabitants of the Americas had no memory of the horse. Therefore, the mounts of the Spaniards who pillaged Central and South America and vainly sought the fabled Seven

Old print shows stack of deer horns taken by the Indians while hunting. Some Indians thought horses were deer without horns.

Cities of Gold terrified the Indians. They not only thought them fearsome but also believed that they were deities.

Even the Aztecs who were as highly civilized as the ancient Egyptians trembled at the sight of the horses of the "Fair Gods." They were sure that the mounted conquistadors were monsters capable of splitting themselves into two parts—man and animal. The Spanish took every advantage of the Indians' awe of horses and warned that the beasts ate humans. When Antonio Espejo explored present-day New Mexico in 1582, he assured the natives that, while he came in peace, he could not promise that his horses would not kill them.

Although the Tlascaltecs of Mexico held that horses were deer that allowed men to ride them, most tribes feared the Spaniards' horses more than they did guns. Nor did the red man lose his belief in the supernatural powers of the horse when the animals became commonplace in New Spain. Coronado reported that during his journey from Mexico to modern Kansas (1539–

1542), daring braves would rub the sweat of his horses on their bodies, hoping to acquire some of the magic of the "big dogs."

There were fifteen hundred head of horses and mules in Coronado's train. With few exceptions they had been raised on ranches in the New World to which the Council of the Indies had sent "selected livestock." Actually, only a small percentage of the Arabian stallions—which were the conquistadors' favorite mounts—and the rugged Barbs from North Africa survived the voyage from Europe. Carried in slings on the decks of sailing ships, many of the horses died from exposure and thirst. Even more were thrown overboard when drinking water ran low on vessels becalmed within thirty degrees north or south of the Equator. Because the residents of New Spain preferred stallions as mounts, mares were the first to be sacrificed. As a result, Spanish sailors called this stretch of the Atlantic the Mares' Gulf. Today, it is known as the Horse Latitudes.

While many of the horses that arrived safely became the mounts of soldiers, a considerable number were allotted to those who had received grants of land for their services to the King of Spain in the New World. Because of ideal climatic conditions, rich grass, and abundant water, these animals throve and, in time, the Spanish dons had so many horses that they were forced to entrust them to the care of their Indian slaves. By this time, the tribesmen had learned—but said nothing of their knowledge—that the Spaniards were not gods, but men, and that horses were not monsters.

Although Indians were allowed to guard horse herds and to curry their masters' mounts, they were forbidden by law to ride. However, while this regulation was enforced in some areas as late as 1611, it was ignored on most ranches. Eventually, the law was repealed with the stipulation that Indians could not use saddles. But few Mexican Indians rode bareback. Legend holds that when Alonzo Martinez, a master saddlemaker, hung a saddletree, the traditional symbol of his craft, above the door of his shop in Mexico City, it disappeared for a night. Shortly afterward, most Indian herdsmen were owners of saddles patterned after Martinez' sign. These saddles, in turn, became the prototype of the stock saddle used by modern cattlemen.

Meanwhile, Spanish officials in South America had disregarded the law forbidding Indians to ride. Thus, by 1580, tribes in Chile, Peru, and Brazil were not only skilled horsemen but also were breeding horses. The Tehuelches of south central Argentina—whose average height of six feet made them the tallest of all Indians—had mastered the horse even earlier. Called the *Patagones* (big feet) by the Spanish, they herded throughout the length of present-day Patagonia and became the ancestors of the gauchos, the famous cowboys of the pampas. The horse also changed the culture of other South American Indians. Among these were the Mbayas, who forced slaves to work their farms while they raided the countryside on horseback.

South American Indians stopped regarding horses as supernatural creatures long before their relations to the north. The Querandis, along with other tribes, dined on mare's meat, shampooed their hair with horses' blood, and used horse bones and fat for fuel. In North America, few tribes relished horsemeat except when starving. Among the exceptions to this general rule were the Apaches. According to an early observer, their appetite for horsemeat gave them such an unpleasant odor that the inhabitants of Sonora claimed their horses would sense this odor and refuse to go forward when they rode near a band of hidden Apaches.

The Spaniards who owned ranches in Mexico and the American Southwest were cruel masters. As a result, abused slaves often stole horses and rode off to freedom. Father Eusebio

An oil by George Catlin (1836). "Smoking Horses" shows the Fox, who are going to war, begging horses from the Saux.

Francisco Kino—the Catholic priest who explored and mapped large areas of New Spain and established missions where he taught the Indians how to raise livestock and crops—reported that 100,000 horses were stolen from Mexican ranches in a single year.

Father Kino's figures are probably exaggerated. But there is no doubt that tremendous numbers of horses were "rustled" by Indians. Through trade and theft, these animals were widely dispersed. For example, Spanish soldiers began reporting bands of mounted Indians as far away as Texas.

Then, in April of 1680, the pueblo dwellers of New Mexico formed an alliance with the Apache and Navajo and revolted. Their uprising was so successful that the Spanish abandoned their ranches and fled in panic. The victorious Indians did not pursue them very far—they were too busy rounding up thousands of horses.

2

"Nothing's more pleasing than to know all the facts."

The pueblo peoples soon discovered that they did not have enough pasturage to support the herds of horses they had stolen from the Spanish. Therefore, they traded many of the animals for the goods of other tribes. While this barter diffused the horse over a wider area, it actually had no effect on the way of life of most North American Indians. Lacking knowledge of the horse, they continued to wander over the countryside and stalk game on foot or to engage in primitive agriculture near their more-or-less permanent settlements.

Long before the discovery of the New World—and for centuries afterward—Indians native to the forested regions of eastern North America lived by a combination of hunting and farming. Certain tribes, after planting fields of beans, corn, squash, and tobacco, left them unattended while they ranged widely, seeking game. Other tribes did not neglect their crops and only hunted close to their villages.

Whether they farmed or not, nearly all red men depended upon animals for food and for the materials from which they fashioned shelters and clothing. Yet very few Indians lived on the Great Plains which teemed with vast herds of buffalo (bison). Only the Crow and the Blackfoot tribes made their homes on the rolling grasslands. They—like the tribes that lived

Before the horse came to America, Indians found it difficult to follow the buffalo (bison). Old print shows brave with game hunted on foot. BELOW: *Oil by Catlin of mounted Caddo (southern Plains) hunting.*

Indians had been using dogs to pull loads for centuries before the missionaries came. Old print shows Mr. West, an English missionary, visiting some Indians five hundred miles from his station at Lake Winnipeg, Canada.

on the fringes of the prairie—did little moving about.

However, when game was scarce or crops failed, these Indians were forced to seek food outside their usual hunting grounds. Since they lacked transportation, they did not travel very far. Moreover, it was an extremely difficult task to pack meat for winter use from remote areas to winter settlements. It was either carried by the hunter's wife, bundled onto a dog's back, or hauled on a travois pulled by a dog.

Made of wood and rawhide, a travois consisted of two poles and crossbars formed in the shape of an A. The point of the A was fastened to a dog's back while the legs dragged on the ground. Loads were lashed to the crossbars. Dogs of northern tribes were capable of pulling heavier loads than those of southern tribes, but the sturdiest dog could not haul more than fifty pounds five or six miles in a day.

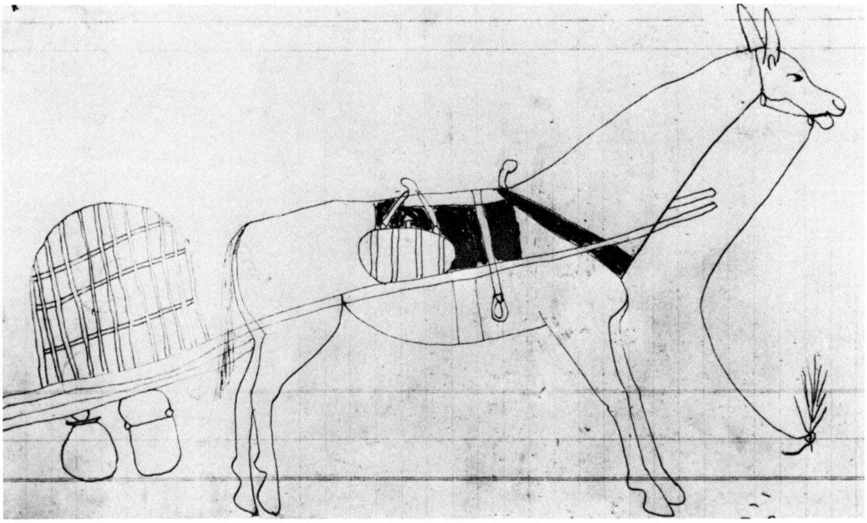

This drawing of a Cheyenne travois with a paunch water container fastened to the saddle was made in 1889 by an unknown Indian artist.

This picture of Stump Horn, one of General W. E. Casey's Cheyenne scouts, and his family was taken in 1899. The bird-cage travois resembles the one above. Note the baby in the cradleboard held by the horse's rider.

Indians living in the region between the Rockies and the Sierra Nevada Mountains also employed dogs as pack animals. They slung baskets on their backs. Until the red man acquired horses, certain of these tribes were the most mobile of all Indians. Because they lived in a region that was too dry for farming and which supported very few wild animals, they tramped along regular routes every year, collecting seeds as they ripened. This method of gathering food is the source of their nickname—the "seed gatherers." Incidentally, because the seed gatherers needed containers to store dried berries, seeds, and nuts for winter use, they mastered the art of basket weaving and, in time, became the most skilled basket makers of all Indians.

Seeds were also harvested by the red men native to the elevated region that comprises most of present-day Nevada and parts of Utah, California, Idaho, Wyoming, and Oregon. These Indians were also hunters. One tribe of their number, the Nez Percé, began trading with horse-owning tribes at a very early date. The Nez Percé not only acquired horses from them but also adopted many of their customs. This pattern would be followed many times—as a tribe learned to ride it borrowed many of the ways of those who provided its first horses.

Meanwhile, the first horses to reach the eastern seaboard of North America in historical times—six mares and two stallions—arrived in Jamestown, Virginia, in 1609. In the years that followed, increasing numbers of horses were imported into the English colonies. Few were pastured in enclosed fields or housed in barns. As a result, by the late seventeenth century, plantation owners were complaining that wild horses were ruining their crops. Actually, these animals were not "wild" but feral—domesticated stock that, when turned out to graze, had strayed and banded together.

Even though feral horses were considered a nuisance, the settlers did not want them to become the property of the Indi-

These ponies, roaming the islands off the coast of Maryland, are descended from Moorish stock. Their forebears were destined for use in the mines of the Viceroy of Peru but swam ashore here from a wreck. Because of lack of crossbreeding, these ponies are representative of the original stock. Early Eastern Indians probably took mounts from the islands as people do today.

ans. In both Virginia and New England, edicts forbade Indians to ride. These were difficult laws to enforce. Unlike southwestern tribes, the Indians of the Atlantic coastline neither feared the horse nor regarded it with superstitious awe. If these tribesmen lived in an area where they could use horses, they did so. Thus, in 1687, the commanding officer of the troops sent to fight the Iroquois wrote to the governor of New France that his foe had "a great number of horses." Most of the animals had been stolen from the farms of the Dutch settlers in the Hudson River Valley in what is now the State of New York.

Meanwhile, Indians in Georgia and South Carolina were riding excellent horses. They had acquired their original stock by trading "white man's goods" for mounts with the Chickasaw who lived in Mississippi. Strangely enough, although no tribe had been more terrified of the Spaniard's horses than the Chickasaw, they quickly mastered the art of horsemanship. They also became expert horse thieves.

Besides stealing horses, the Chickasaw raised them. By selective breeding, they eventually developed the "Chickasaw horse." Small, exceptionally well-proportioned, active, alert, and attractive, it was highly regarded by both whites and Indians for its long stride and endurance.

While the Chickasaw willingly bartered horses for the goods of other tribes, they rarely consented to trade with white men. However, during the wars fought in the New World between England and France, the Chickasaw—who were allies of the English—did do business with the French. They exchanged captive Frenchmen for horses. But they would only accept stock that would improve their herds.

In 1775, James Adair, an Indian trader, visited the Choctaw and Cherokee and reported, ". . . almost everyone hath horses, from two to a dozen . . . the Cherokee a prodigious number." While it is very likely that both the Choctaw and the Cherokee

Artistic conception of the Chickasaw horse by Sam Savitt, well known for his drawings of horses.

received their first horses from the Chickasaw, there are other possibilities. They could have captured feral horses or traded for mounts with Indians living farther south. The latter, in turn, had procured their horses from Indians who raided Spanish ranches.

It is relatively easy to trace the adoption of the horse by eastern tribes. But no one knows when the Indians living west of the Mississippi River first acquired mounts. Nevertheless, it has been established that the red men who lived on the Great Plains and in the land of plateaus that lies between Idaho's Wasatch Range and the Sierra Nevada Mountains in eastern California were riding long before their first recorded contact with the white man.

Old print of an Arabian horse, ancestor of the horses the Indians rode

Legend holds that both Plains and Plateau Indians got their first steeds by taming mustangs. Traditionally, the mustangs were the descendants of horses that had either strayed away from, or had been abandoned by, De Soto's and Coronado's expeditions. Fact disproves both legend and tradition. All of De Soto's horses were killed by hostile tribesmen. Furthermore, out of the 558 horses listed on Coronado's muster roll, only two were mares and there is no mention of either being lost in the detailed chronicle of his adventures.

Even if one assumes that a stallion from De Soto's herd survived and that Coronado's animals included an unrecorded mare, the chance of the two meeting and mating somewhere on the Great Plains is most improbable. Nor is it biologically possible for a single pair of horses to be the sole ancestors of the thousands of "broomtails" that once ranged the grasslands of North America.

Actually, the original "wild horses" of the Plains were the two breeds introduced into the New World by the Spanish—Arabians and Barbs. While only a few of these horses had strayed from explorer's camps or ranches, thousands of them had galloped to freedom when the Indians revolted in 1680 and drove the Spanish out of New Mexico. In time, the Arabians and Barbs were joined by bigger and heavier Dutch, English, and French horses that had escaped from wagon trains rolling westward.

The Spanish purebreds and the stock from Northern Europe interbred. Eventually, their offspring mated with the horses of hybrid ancestry that broke away from the picket lines of the cavalry assigned to subdue the Indians.

Out of these matings came the mustang. There were so many

Mustang in shaggy winter coat gallops across the Plains.

Northern Indians obtained horses that had been passed from tribe to tribe from the Spanish settlements to the south. A Potawatomi family on horseback, sketched by German painter Rudolph Friederich Kurz, who roamed the western part of North America from 1846 to 1852. Note the details of the picture, including horses' equipment.

of these mongrel horses that they darkened the Plains. Meanwhile, the purebred descendants of the Spanish Barbs and Arabians almost became extinct. Today, while a few roam on ranches in the Southwest, none are found in the wild.

The red man did not begin to domesticate wild horses in any great number until after 1800. If, as indicated, certain Plains and Plateau tribes were riding long before that date, their horses must have come from the Spanish settlements to the south, the animals being passed northward from tribe to tribe.

Eventually, horses stolen in New Spain were transferred from owner to owner along well-defined trade routes. Two of these routes ended at the villages of the Arikara, Hidatsa, and

Mandan along the Missouri River where, for centuries, nomadic tribes had exchanged pelts and dried buffalo meat for agricultural products. From these trading centers, horses went out to Indians living north and east of the Missouri who also came to the "trading fairs" held near the villages.

It was not unusual for several thousand tribesmen to take part in one of these events. Pierre La Verendrye attended one in 1739 and noted:

> . . . every year in the beginning of June there arrive at the great fort on the bank of the river of the Mandan, several savage tribes which use the horse and carry on a trade with them; that they bring dressed skins trimmed and ornamented with plummage and porcupine quills, painted in various colors, also white buffalo skins, and that the Mandan give them in exchange grain and beans, of which they have an ample supply.

Original of this drawing showing Flathead Indians crossing a stream with the assistance of their mounts was made by Gustavus Sohon prior to 1862. The warrior in the foreground is holding onto his horse's tail.

Pictograph of horse stealing drawn by Jaw.

Both Plains and Plateau Indians continued to barter for mounts long after they learned to capture and break wild horses. They found domesticated animals far easier to train. But as the Plains Indians became more and more dependent upon the horse they discovered that they could not possibly accumulate sufficient goods to barter for all the trained horses they desired.

However, the tribesmen of the Plains developed a method of acquiring mounts that not only cost them nothing but also enabled young men to display their bravery. They stole the horses of their neighbors. While this practice achieved its two aims, it also led to the intertribal warfare that swept across the Plains during the late eighteenth and early nineteenth centuries.

3

"All new things are apt to please."

A number of northern tribes abandoned their traditional hunting grounds and farmlands and migrated to the Great Plains after acquiring the horse. They were lured onto the prairie because the horse not only made it possible for them to follow the buffalo for hundreds of miles during the warm months and secure an abundance of food for use then but also allowed them to accumulate meat to preserve for winter use.

Thus the horse created a new type of Indian—a wanderer who was completely dependent upon the buffalo for food, clothing, and shelter and whose rituals and religion reflected his respect for the animal he hunted. Because the horse peopled the prairie and changed so many age-old customs, anthropologists—students of the various races of man—label the years between the Plains Indians' first use of the horse and the extermination of the buffalo herds the "Horse Culture Period."

Before this culture was firmly established, certain newcomers to the Plains regarded horses as some sort of huge dog. To the Assiniboin the horse was the "great dog"; the Blackfoot called it "elk-dog"; while the Sioux, convinced that the horse was of divine origin, named it *hunka-a-wakan*—"medicine dog."

The Plains Indians quickly learned that horses were far more efficient at transporting household goods and freshly killed game than dogs. Not only could a horse drawing a travois haul a 200-pound load but also it could cover twice the distance in a day than a dog pulling far less weight.

Actually, certain Plains Indians employed the horse-drawn travois before they learned to ride. While the Blackfoot tribe was probably the first to harness a horse to a travois, practically every buffalo-hunting tribe had its own variant of the vehicle. But irrespective of the size, shape, and construction of the loading platform, the length of the poles, or the method used to hitch the horse, every travois pulled by a horse was merely an enlarged version of the original A-shaped device.

At first, the same horses were used for both packing and riding. Then, as their herds increased, the Plains Indians selected their swiftest mounts and painstakingly trained them to hunt.

This reproduction of the original oil by Seth Eastman of "Sioux Indians Breaking Up Camp" is courtesy of the Museum of Fine Arts, Boston, M. and M. Karolik Collection. It was painted before 1848. Note the travois.

Astride a "buffalo runner," a brave would pick out a particular buffalo in a herd and race neck and neck with it until in a position to shoot an arrow into a vulnerable spot. As the bow twanged, the horse automatically turned away to avoid colliding with the animal as it staggered and fell.

A well-trained buffalo runner needed no guidance. When Lewis and Clark trekked across the Great Plains, they discovered that as soon as certain horses they had purchased from friendly Indians scented buffalo, they galloped toward them. Therefore, they assigned one of their party to ride ahead and drive off any buffalo he encountered.

Not every brave had the ability and patience to school a buffalo runner. Nor could such horses be secured easily in trade. They were seldom bartered. When they were, a high value was placed on them. The only item a Hidatsa would accept in exchange for one was a white buffalo skin—a pelt all Plains Indians believed had magical powers.

During the early years of the Horse Culture Period, buffalo runners were relatively rare in some tribes. There were so few

Three mounted Cree sketched by Kurz.

of them among the Plains Cree that their owners—whose successful hunts enabled them to supply others with meat—became tribal leaders. However, any horse, whether specially trained or merely broken to ride, made hunting buffalo far easier. Before mastering the horse, the Indians had killed buffalo by approaching the animals on foot, frightening them by waving blankets, and causing them to stampede over a cliff; by luring their quarry into bush or rock corrals; or by engaging in a surround. The latter consisted of a group of hunters encircling several hundred buffalo and forcing them to mill about until the beasts were so exhausted that they could be shot at close range.

Whether they rode run-of-the-herd mounts or buffalo runners, the Plains Indians engaged in various ceremonies designed to make their horses run faster. They also ritually blew herbs and the smoke from the dried leaves and roots of "magic" plants into the animals' noses and dosed them with concoctions compounded by the leaders of the secret cults who preserved the mysteries of "horse medicine."

Besides employing potions to increase their horses' speed, the Plains Indians also slit their mounts' nostrils. Peter Pond, who lived with the Dakota Sioux in 1745, reported:

> In order to have there Horsis Long Winded they Slit their Noses up to the Grissel of thare head which Make them Breath verey freely, I Have Sean them run with those of Naturall Nostrals and In Apearantley Not the Least Out of Breath.

Along with swiftness, the Plains Indians demanded great endurance from the horses they used for hunting. The Mandan chased buffalo day and night without allowing their mounts to rest or eat, while the Sioux never watered their horses until the morning after a hunt. Yet, despite this cruelty, most tribes

Lithograph from a painting by John Mix Stanley, September, 1853, of mounted Indians pursuing the buffalo

Catlin's oil, "Buffalo Chase with Bows and Lances"

treated their horses kindly. For example, the Shoshoni—along with others—shod their horses with moccasins fashioned from untanned buffalo hide to protect their hoofs.

"The red knights of the Plains" dominated the prairies until the invention of the repeating rifle. Armed with a short bow—which was easy for a mounted man to handle—and carrying up to one hundred arrows in his quiver, a warrior was more than a match for an enemy firing a single-shot gun. In the time it took to measure and pour powder, ram the ball down the barrel, and adjust the flintlock, an Indian could release twenty arrows. Meanwhile, his charging horse instantly responded to signals given by its rider's legs.

Not only did the weaving and wheeling of a well-trained war horse make a warrior difficult to hit but also man and mount seemed to blend into one during a battle. George Catlin, the famous artist who visited most Plains tribes during the early nineteenth century, was amazed at their horsemanship when charging a foe. Catlin was particularly impressed with the Comanche. According to Catlin, a Comanche brave could:

. . . drop his body upon the side of his horse, effectively screened from his enemies' weapons as he (lies) in a horizontal position behind the body of his horse, with his heel hanging down over the horse's back: by which he has the power of throwing himself up again, and changing to the other side of the horse if necessary.

In this wonderful condition, he will hang whilst his horse is at the

Catlin painted "Comanche Feats of Horsemanship" in 1834. Note the braves hanging by their heels while carrying shields, bows and arrows, and long lances, just as Catlin described in his writing.

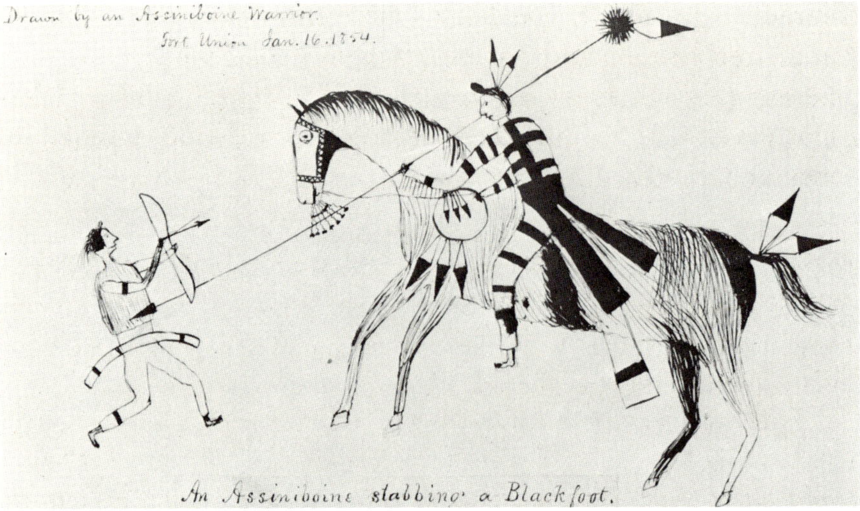

fullest speed, carrying with him his bow and shield, and also his long lance of fourteen feet in length, all or either of which he will wield upon his enemy as he passes; rising and throwing his arrows over the horse's back, or with ease and equal success under the horse's neck.

War horses were trained in mock battles. They were also taught to "dance" and to rear and neigh loudly. Dancing made horses difficult targets—Indians always shot first at a horse rather than its rider—while rearing and neighing were thought to frighten foes. The Sioux and other tribes schooled their war horses to jump over fallen opponents. Such a leap "counted coup," just as if the enemy had been actually touched in hand-to-hand combat—an act considered by the red man to be the highest form of bravery.

Braves who counted coup (the word comes from the French "to hit") had the right to paint a red hand on their horses or to wear a coup feather. If the latter was notched, it signified that the brave's horse had been wounded in battle.

A warrior could also count coup if he rescued a dishorsed

comrade. As a result, war horses were trained to carry double. But a tired horse could not bear a heavy load while galloping. Therefore, war horses were ridden only in actual combat. Warriors traveled to a battlefield astride less valuable animals to conserve the strength of their best mounts. Incidentally, in the early years of cavalry warfare on the Plains, a number of tribes imitated the armor of the Spanish by fashioning protective devices for both their horses and themselves from buffalo hide. They also copied the Spanish habit of mounting a horse from the right side.

Excluding buffalo hunting, war was the most important activity of the Plains Indians. But they did not fight for land, wealth, or slaves. Their constant skirmishes with their neighbors were motivated by every brave's desire to gain personal glory. Mounted on a trained war horse, an individual could perform far more daring deeds than an unmounted warrior. Therefore, even when faced with starvation, a Plains Indian hesitated to swap his charger for food.

Because of the danger of losing a war horse by theft, prized

"Comanche Lancing an Osage" was painted by Catlin in 1834.

Artistic conception of a lone Indian creeping up to steal a tethered buffalo runner

steeds were often tethered to the doorways of their owners' dwellings. When on the march, warriors slept with their horses tied to their wrists with a hair rope.

No individuals were more respected by the Plains Indians than successful horse thieves. The members of the Blackfoot tribe were an exception. This is because they "took it for granted that by the time their men were warriors they would have learned how to be expert horse raiders."

While the more horses a brave stole the higher his position in the community, most tribes discounted his achievements if he killed during a raiding expedition. No Cree could count coup for stealing horses unless he had been in danger of getting caught. The Crow—who considered recapturing stolen horses more valorous than purloining new ones—paid more honor to those who made off with picketed horses than to men who drove off an unattended herd.

Horse raiding parties were composed of volunteers. They

often set out on foot, confident that they would ride back. Mounted thieves approached the camp they planned to rob on horseback, dismounted, left their horses in charge of a boy, and walked the rest of the way.

Before hiding so that they could pick out the finest horses and plan their attack without being observed, Indians always washed thoroughly with sand and water. This was to prevent the animals they intended to steal from scenting the odor of strange horses on their bodies. If this happened the frightened, restless herd would warn its owners.

While an extremely bold brave might ride into a village as if he belonged to it and manage to escape with a prized horse, most raids took place just before dawn. They were completely silent operations that had been planned down to the last detail. Thus, an experienced horse thief could crawl among a dozen sleeping men, "each with his horse tied to his wrist with a lariat, cut off the rope within six feet of a sleeper's person, and get off with the horse without waking a soul."

Sioux braves—who thought horse stealing the most exciting of sports—boasted of their ability to sneak into another tribe's encampment and drive away the mounts of famous warriors by chanting:

Reproduction of a Frederic Remington canvas painted about 1890 shows a lone Indian scout and his mount.

This reproduction of Alfred Jacob Miller's "Beating a Retreat" courtesy of the Museum of Fine Arts, Boston, Massachusetts, M. and M. Karolik Collection. The fine heads of the steeds with small pricked ears and dished faces are Arabian.

Indians got plenty of practice for horse-stealing raids by racing their mounts. Taken from the C.M. Russell BOYHOOD SKETCHBOOK, *courtesy Treasure Products, Inc., Bozeman, Montana.*

You must watch your horse.
A horse thief often I am.

Despite this conceit, members of every raiding party realized that, unless they escaped with *all* the mounts owned by a village, there would be a pursuit and the chase could last for several weeks. Moreover, the thieves knew that if they were overtaken they would be killed.

High-ranking officers of the United States Cavalry who were commissioned to bring peace to the Frontier soon discovered that the horse was the cause and means of the constant warfare on the Plains. They also learned that one of the reasons some tribes refused to meet and discuss a treaty of peace was the fear that their horses would be stolen during the negotiations. This is why the Comanche who were among the most accomplished of horse thieves did not join the Great Council of 1851 called by the United States Government. The Comanche refused to attend, despite the promise of many gifts from the Great White Father. Their excuse was that they had "too many good horses to risk them among such thieves as the Sioux and Crow."

Copy of Gustavus Sohon's "The Bloods in Council" (1855) shows Blackfeet riding to meet representatives of the "Great White Father."

4

"Wealth . . . means power . . . it means liberty."

Horses represented wealth to the Plains Indians. Since none were tribally owned, the possession of a large herd gave a family a social status best compared to that held by modern two- and three-car families.

Besides making their owners important tribal figures, horses also insured them a constant supply of food. Even if a horse owner was too old to chase buffalo, he could get all the meat he wanted by lending his mount to a younger man who repaid him by sharing his kill. Actually, individuals who borrowed horses usually returned them with a gift. But they were not required to show their appreciation. The Plains Indians considered anyone who owned horses and did not share them very selfish.

Actually, a man's prestige did not depend so much on the size of his horse herd but on the number of horses he gave away. Thus, since horses were regarded as the most valuable of gifts, individuals with large herds could easily acquire the reputation of being generous. They also could secure the special attention of the shamans who interpreted dreams, cured sicknesses, and provided protective amulets and medicine-pipe bundles. The Sarcee paid six or eight horses for the latter and gave a shaman a horse for naming a child.

Certain Plains Indians distributed ponies to their friends

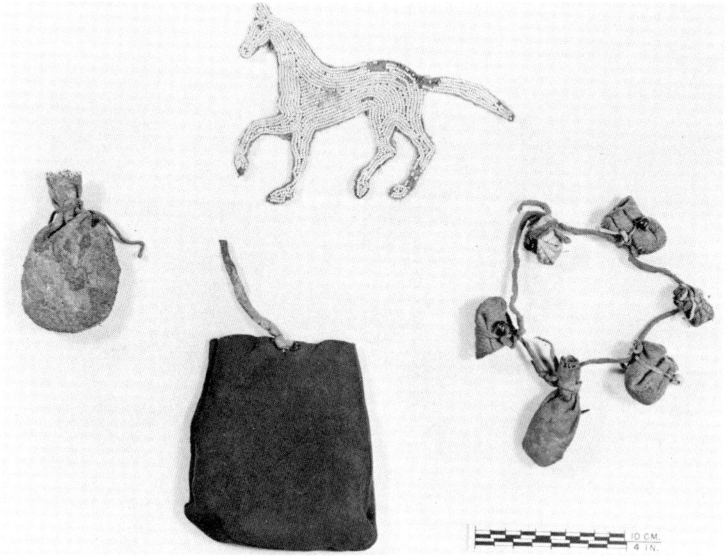

Part of the contents of the horse medicine bundle of Wallace Night Gun, a Blackfoot shaman. The bag on the left holds the beaded horse fetish and the other two pouches hold secret potions for curing sick horses and capturing mustangs.

when a son was born to them. When a Sioux girl was ready for marriage, her father held a party. The maiden threw a red ball among the guests, and the person who caught it was given a horse. She continued to toss the ball until the supply of horses was exhausted.

Throughout the Plains, horses were the recognized medium of exchange. Their value in trade generally depended upon an individual's need of a mount and the number of available horses. The Wichita who lived in a treeless area gladly swapped one horse for five lodgepoles. The Crow, who were very shrewd traders, disposed of their horses for twice what they had paid for them. On the other hand, the Flathead bartered horses "for trifles," according to one historian. When Lewis and Clark dealt with the Shoshoni, they gave "an ax, a handkerchief, and a little paint" for a horse. But the Mandan, who owned relatively few horses, demanded much more from fur trader Francois Laroque.

The woman in this Kurz sketch is an Iowa but her saddle is typical of the one used by women of all tribes. In the upper left of sketch are three Crow saddlebags.

He paid "a gun with balls, one fanel Robe, one shirt, one half axe" and several other items, including a "Wampoon shell," for a mount.

Horse raiding parties were frequently composed of young men seeking horses in order to purchase a wife. Blackfoot, Blood, and Piegan families demanded from one to twenty horses for a maiden, depending upon her beauty and disposition. Other tribes required a suitor to offer as many as ten horses for a bride. The animals were not considered a payment but positive proof of the would-be groom's wealth.

Maidens had no rights to the horses paid for them. For example, among the Assiniboin, the horses went to the girl's oldest brother. However, in several tribes women owned horses. They either received them as gifts from relatives or from their husbands' family. Cree custom decreed that a woman's horses were her personal property and, even if her spouse cared for them, she alone could dispose of the animals. Piegan braves who lost their own horses when gambling knew that they would be censured by tribal leaders if they attempted to recoup by betting their wives' mounts.

Meanwhile, the horse improved the status of Indian women. Their age-old chore of carrying burdens from one campsite to another became the task of horses trained to the travois. When horses became plentiful, women also rode as tribes followed the buffalo herds. Women whose husbands could not provide them with mounts were pitied by all and were lent horses.

Indian women never became as skilled in riding as Indian men. But some were outstanding. This is particularly true of Comanche, Crow, Flathead, and Shoshoni women. The latter even chased mustangs and roped them, while Flathead women engaged in horse racing against men.

When a woman died, her horses became the property of her husband. But the disposal of a dead warrior's horses varied from tribe to tribe. When an Assiniboin bachelor died, all his horses were herded onto the prairie and left to roam at will, but when a married man died, only his finest mounts were given their freedom.

Usually, horses were killed at a brave's funeral so that he

Blackfoot Pinto bears a woman's saddle and decorated equipment.

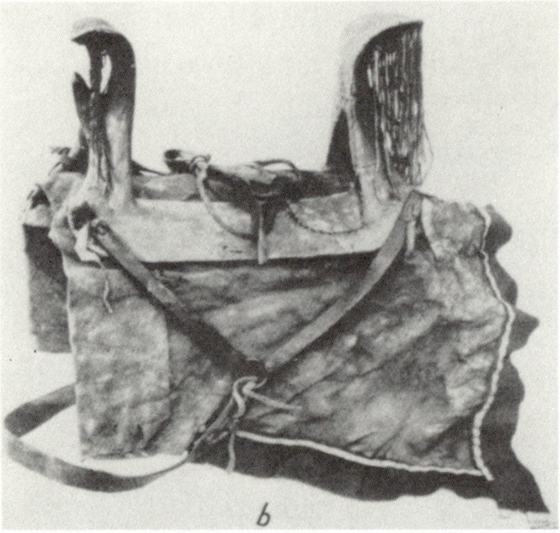

A woman's "wood saddle," Blood Indians

would be able to ride in the land of the spirits. Most tribes only destroyed the dead man's favorite horse. However, the number of horses sacrificed by the Blackfoot depended upon the deceased's prestige. As many as 150 animals might be killed to honor a chief but the majority of warriors went riding into eternity with twenty horses.

When death called a Sioux to ride down the "Walking Trail of Spirits," he was dressed in his finest regalia, wrapped in a buffalo robe, and his body, surrounded by his most cherished possessions, was placed on a scaffold.

Meanwhile, a male relative had been busy painting red blotches over the dead man's horse and covering it with a blanket. A close friend of the deceased then led the animal to the foot of the scaffold where he said to it, "Grandfather, your owner thought a great deal of you and now he is dead. He wants to take you with him so go joyfully."

As he finished addressing the horse, he shot it at close range so that death was instant and painless. The animal's tail was then cut off and attached to a pole at the front of the scaffold to which the dead man's weapons, coup stick, and medicine pouch were fastened.

5

"Some things are bred in the bone."

Of all the peoples who have galloped through history, none have had greater mastery of the horse than the Plains Indians. One of the reasons is that they were associated with horses from birth. Flathead children were rocked to sleep by the swaying of their cradles which were tied to horses, while Crow toddlers rode from camp to camp strapped to saddles. Although the saddles had high backs and fronts to prevent the youngsters from falling, the children could pretend that they were brave warriors because each had a whip strapped to his wrist.

Between the ages of four or five, when a child was big enough to straddle a mount, he received his first formal riding instruction. In some tribes boys were taught by their fathers or a male relative, girls by their mothers. Either parent did the teaching in other tribes. A gentle horse was always used—Blackfoot women employed a docile horse trained to pull a travois. If a family did not own a suitable horse, it borrowed one.

At first the instructor, afoot or astride another mount, led the novices through the village at a slow walk. As the children gained experience and confidence, the pace was increased and they learned to use reins and to control a horse. By the time youngsters were seven years old they usually were excellent riders although they needed a short rawhide rope woven into a

Indian boys of the Plains would have enjoyed working this Pony of the Americas stud as much as this boy of today does.

horse's mane to pull themselves onto the animal's back.

After learning to ride, boys were taught to lock their legs around a galloping horse's neck, swing their bodies down, and shoot at a target from under their mount's neck. They also learned to leap on a charging horse, gallop to a comrade sprawled on the ground as if he were wounded, lift him up, and ride on without stopping. Meanwhile, boys constantly practiced throwing the lariat and became as proficient in roping as they were in riding.

Boys paid for their lessons by guarding horse herds. They got up before daybreak, went to the night pasture, drove the animals to water, then hazed them into the encampment. After the adults chose the mounts they wanted, the rest of the herd was turned out to graze. The herders watered the horses again at noon and just before taking them to the night pasture. Their last task was to hobble the lead mare to prevent the herd from straying.

Herds were not guarded at night except when there was reason to believe they were in danger. However, while all the horses belonging to a village grazed together during the day, they were scattered over a much larger area at night to lessen the chances of all being stolen. Incidentally, while it was the chief's duty to choose campsites that provided ample pasturage, each family was responsible for its own horses.

Except when lightning, a prairie fire, or wolves stampeded a horse herd or the shrieking of a startled bird revealed that horse thieves were near, the boys had little to do. To pass the time they rode warrior's mounts and raced horses—usually without permission—or accepted dares to ride an untamed horse. While some youngsters lacked the necessary courage to break horses, many teen-agers became such expert horse trainers that they schooled mounts for their elders.

Boys of the Blackfoot tribe often broke horses in water. Two of them would mount a horse, the front rider leading a bronco with a rope, and enter a pond or stream. When the water was up to the animals' shoulders, the first boy took up the slack on the lead rope, thus enabling his companion to jump onto the untamed horse. As he did so, the rope was dropped and the tame horse ridden out of the water. Because the bronco could not get a firm footing, its attempts to buck off its rider failed and the animal soon exhausted itself and accepted the weight on its back.

Horses broken by Gros Ventre boys in the Missouri River did little bucking. The herds of this tribe were driven into the water every day and the boys would swim beside them, patting their necks and clambering over their backs. As a result, the horses became accustomed to a human's mounting them. Actually, no herders had a closer relationship with their charges than Gros

A Kurz sketch of Gros Ventre braves on their favorite mounts. Note clipped mane and decorative neck strap on the horse at left.

Ventre boys. Thus, when a herd became restless, they quieted it by singing:

> You are my gods,
> I take good care of you.

Besides breaking horses to ride, boys also assisted in the training of the large, sturdy animals that served as draft horses. One common method was to tie a buffalo hide just behind the horse's legs by two long lines which were fastened to either side of a rawhide rope around the animal's neck. One to three boys rode on the hide as a man led the horse over smooth ground. Because of the length of the ropes, the boys were in no danger of being kicked, but spills were frequent as the horse often bolted. In time, however, it became accustomed to the load behind and could be safely harnessed to a travois.

While older teen-agers were delighted when asked by an adult to break a horse, the highest honor a young man who was adept at handling horses could receive was to be invited to join one of the horse medicine cults. This meant that he could take part in the horse dance and also learn the secret formulas that cured sick horses. Those that had such knowledge and knew the rituals that supposedly influenced the actions of horses were highly regarded by all Plains Indians.

Members of the horse medicine cults could prescribe for sick and ailing animals and prepare potions that assured warriors their mounts would never falter. But they had no magic concoction that protected horses from the blizzards that covered the Plains with a thick blanket of snow. Nor could the rites of the horse medicine men guarantee that a tribe's horses would be able to paw through encrusted snow, reach the withered grass below, and survive until spring.

In the early 1930's, an Indian found a use for his horses of which the early Plains tribes could never have dreamed. From the photo archive of St. Francis Indian Mission to the Rosebud Sioux, St. Francis, South Dakota; photo by Reverend Eugene Buechel, S.J.

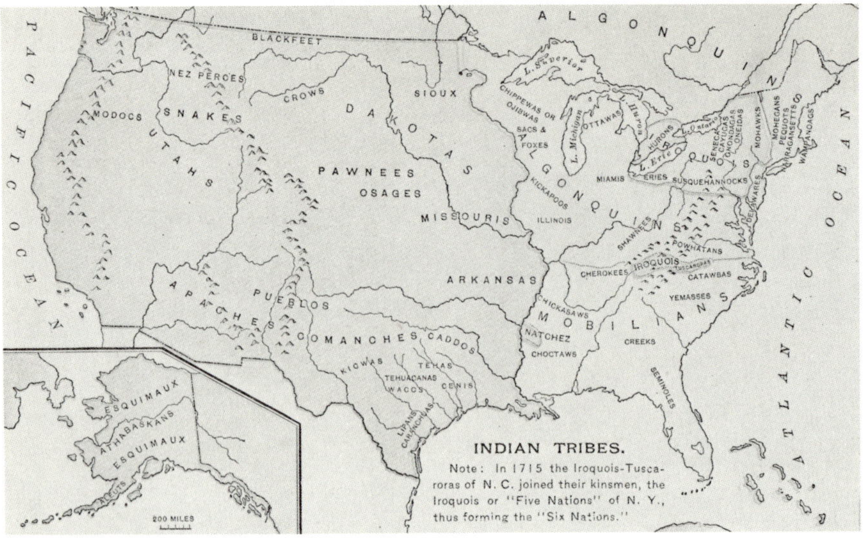

Old map shows location of some of the tribes.

Paul Kane painted a horserace held by the Blackfoot Indians, 1848. The Plains Indians designated some months by the condition of their mounts, so important was the horse to them.

Many Plains Indians, fearful of losing their best mounts through starvation or freezing, kept the animals in their dwellings on winter nights. During the day they pastured them in the shelter of cottonwood thickets. There, the animals fed on dry grass exposed by the constant winds or nibbled on cottonwood boughs.

Cottonwood kept the northern Plains Indians' horses alive during the winter. While some tribes gathered small amounts of grass for winter forage in the fall, there was no actual haying on the prairie before the coming of white settlers. Although the red men of Texas supplied their mounts with maize (corn) in the winter, northern tribes did not. In fact, when Meriwether Lewis offered the horses of his Mandan hosts buckets of bran, they refused it. This prompted him to record, "They make it an invariable rule to put their horses in their lodges at night. In this situation, the only food of the horse consists of a few sticks of cottonwood, from the size of a man's finger to that of his arm."

Despite the lack of nourishment furnished by their winter diet, most of the horses stabled in huts, lodges, or sheds survived. So did a surprising number of the animals left to fend for themselves. Standing belly deep in the snow, they managed to find enough dried grass or cottonwood bark to keep them alive. But long before the arrival of spring they were thin and weak.

As the Plains turned green with new vegetation, the half-starved horses put on weight and regained strength. Nevertheless, many did not live until June, the month known to the Cheyenne as "the time horses get fat." After weeks of early warm spring weather, sudden storms often dumped a foot or more of snow on the Plains and temperatures dropped to well below freezing. As a result, entire herds of horses died. This is why the Mandan called March and April "the horses' winter."

6

"In number as sand and dust."

Despite the losses they suffered every winter, the Plains Indians' horse herds increased over the years. The thousands of mustangs that grazed on the prairie provided them with a seemingly inexhaustible source of mounts. Actually, in some areas there were far more wild horses than buffalo.

Today, only a few wild horses are recognized by the Spanish Mustang Registry as being purebred descendants of the mounts of the conquistadors. But for decades nearly all free-running mustangs of the Plains displayed the traits and conformation of their remote ancestors, the animals stolen from ranches in New Spain. Then, as noted, the pure blood of the Spanish invaders' Arabians and Barbs became mixed with that of other breeds—Chickasaw horses acquired through barter, animals taken from English and French outposts, wagon trains, and picket lines that had descended from the mixing of the blood lines of Thoroughbreds, Morgans, Quarter Horses, heavy draft breeds, and others. Because the captured horses were often unable to keep up with the fleet mounts ridden by their captors during the chases that usually followed a successful raid on a settlement, they were frequently released. While the Indians hoped to recapture the stolen horses after eluding their pursuers, the animals could not always be found. Some made their way back to their home pas-

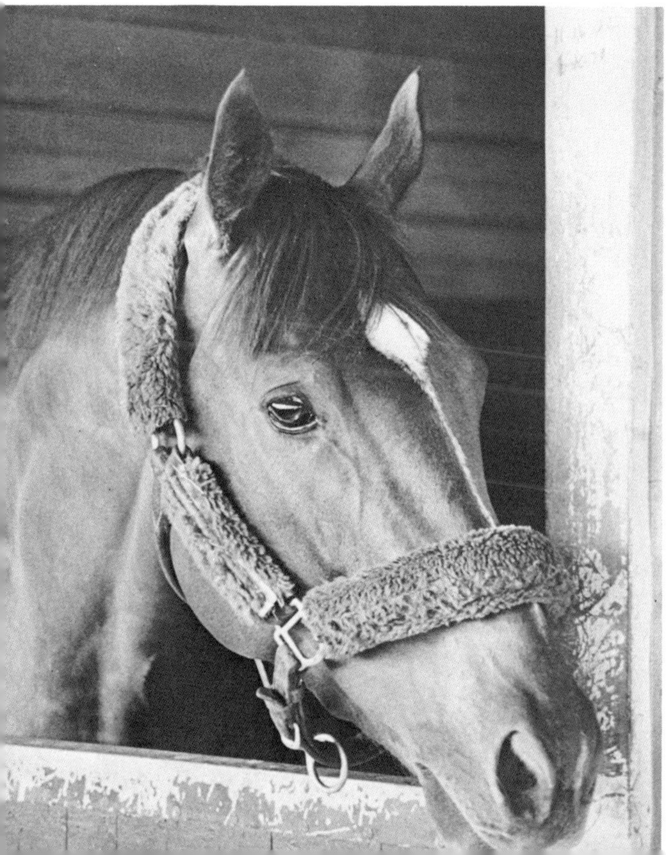

ABOVE: *Painting shows model conformation of the Quarter Horse.*

LEFT: *Secretariat, one of the most loved and well known of Thoroughbreds.*

Both breeds contributed their bloodlines to the horses ridden by the Indians.

The mustang, a crossbreed, is tough enough to survive in the wild.

tures, but others eventually joined bands of wild horses that had never known halter or harness and mated with them.

Tough and agile, the mustang that came out of this maze of crossbreeding prospered despite predators, prairie fires, drought, and bitter winters. It is estimated that a million mustangs ranged in Texas during the last years of the eighteenth century and the first decades of the nineteenth century. Father Morfi, an early missionary, reported to his superiors in 1777 that "bands of wild horses were so abundant that their trails made the country, utterly uninhabited by people, like as if it were the most populated in the world." Some years later, Zebulon Pike, discoverer of the peak that bears his name, was unable to estimate the number of mustangs he encountered while exploring what is now Colorado.

Meanwhile, thousands of wild horses were roaming the grasslands of South America. Some of these animals were the descendents of the large herd Pedro de Mendoza "left behind in the place called Buenos Aires." But the ancestry of the majority was the breeding stock sent to ranches and military outposts by the Spanish authorities in Peru, the center for the distribution of horses throughout South America in the sixteenth century.

Actually, there were far more wild horses on the Argentine pampas than on the Great Plains. But there were more than enough mustangs ranging the northern prairies to satisfy the Indians' compulsion to own as many horses as possible. In addition to the bands that spread over Texas, approximately a million other mustangs—the word is a corruption of the Spanish *mestengos*, a term applied to sheep that strayed while being driven to pasture—inhabited the area bounded by the Missis-

A Currier and Ives print of Catlin's sketch of one of the "numerous bands of wild horses" he saw while he was roaming the Plains.

sippi River on the east, California on the west, and Saskatchewan on the north.

Led by powerful stallions, mustangs ran in small bands. Although a band's home territory usually covered about twenty square miles, several bands often shared areas where grass and water were plentiful and shelter from storms was easily found. Lieutenant Ulysses S. Grant, who was to gain fame as leader of the Union Army during the War Between the States, was amazed at the number of mustangs he saw in such a region while on patrol. When making his report, Grant claimed that he had seen so many wild horses that he doubted "if all of them could be corralled in the State of Rhode Island."

When and where a mustang was first roped by an Indian is unknown. While there is ample evidence that the red man was taught to throw the lariat by Spanish ranchers, strangely enough, the first authenticated report of Indians using the lasso comes from the northern Plains—Lewis and Clark's statement

Mustangs run in small bands led by a stallion.

Note the beautiful heads Kurz drew (1851) on this sketch of a Gros Ventre brave chasing wild horses.

that the Shoshoni were experts "at casting the cord." Equally odd is the fact that, long before roping mustangs was a common practice among the Plains Indians, the Sioux pictograph for a wild horse was a lasso.

Although most Plains tribes eventually practiced roping—a few tribes preferred snaring wild horses with a flexible willow loop fastened to a pole—only outstanding animals were lassoed. Far more mustangs were captured by other methods—blocking the entrances of canyons and passes, driving a band into a camouflaged pen, chasing wild horses until they were exhausted, and by surrounds. A special technique was employed in the winter when mustangs were weak from lack of food. Mounted on relays of fast horses, Indian mustangers would force a band to keep moving until it became so weary that the animals floun-

While making this drawing, Catlin wrote in his journal that the Indians took great care "not to subdue the spirit of the animal" when breaking a horse. Note the brave in the background "casting a cord."

dered in the snow. Incidentally, the latter technique is still used by those who prey on the fast-dwindling bands of wild horses

After the bow gave way to the gun, the prairie dwellers often attempted to capture an extraordinary fine mustang by "creasing"—shooting so that the bullet merely stunned the animal. But, more often than not, the horse was killed.

The Cayuse were such outstanding mustangers that the name of this tribe has become a synonym for "horse" throughout the American West. But no Indians were more adept at capturing wild horses than the Crow. It is estimated that they added at least ten thousand mustangs to their herds. Other tribes also rounded up large numbers. The Kiowa presented the Cheyenne with so many wild horses at the Great Peace of 1844 that the latter did not have enough ropes to lead the animals back to their encampments. But this did not stop the Cheyenne from continuing to catch mustangs. Meanwhile, the Sioux were also actively engaged in mustanging. While it is impossible even to guess the number of wild horses captured by the Sioux and Cheyenne, the total count must have been enormous. Nor is there any doubt that both these tribes excelled in training mustangs to serve as war horses. Proof is furnished by the fact that the approximately five thousand Sioux and Cheyenne warriors who charged General George A. Custer at the Battle of the Little Big Horn in June, 1876, were mounted on mustangs.

Generally speaking, neither mustangs nor domestic stock were broken until the animals were three years old. While cer-

A Cree and his horse herd, sketch by Kurz

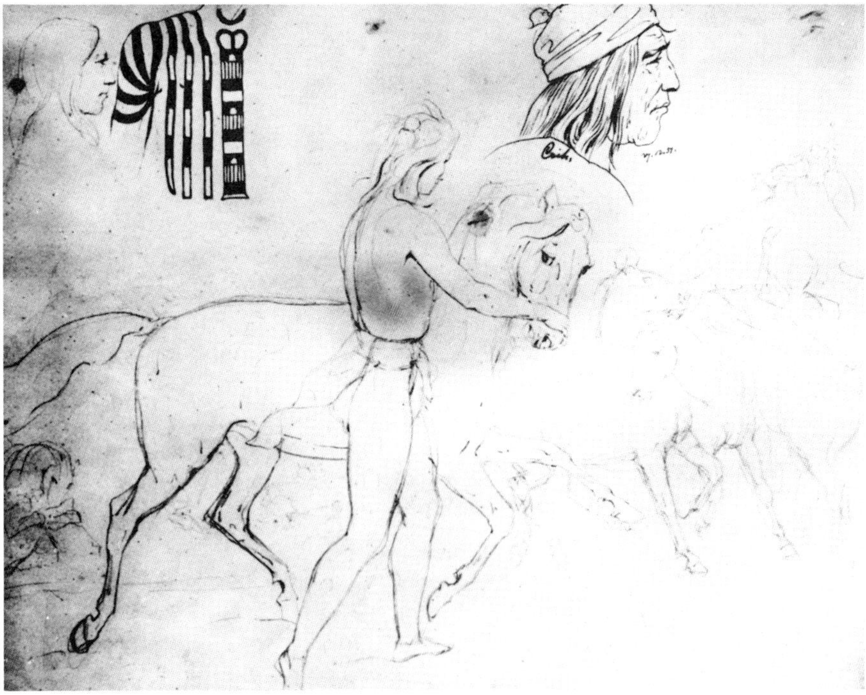

A page from Kurz sketchbook gives his impressions of the Indian's way with horses.

tain tribes used brutal methods to train horses, the majority tried not to break the animals' spirit.

No horse trainers were more patient than the Blackfoot of Canada. When a member of this tribe wished to master a horse, he had four assistants hold it with a rope while he approached the animal, mumbling soothing sounds. When the frightened horse stopped struggling, the trainer slowly passed a blanket in front of its nose to accustom the animal to human scent.

A rawhide halter was then fastened around the muzzle and behind the ears in such a way that, whenever the horse tossed its head, the rawhide tightened and caused pain. When this device was in place, the trainer, still murmuring softly, ran his hands lightly over the horse's body. Then, after gently stroking the animal with the blanket, he threw it across its back. If the blanket was bucked off, it was replaced.

When the horse finally accepted the blanket, the trainer placed his elbows upon it and alternately raised and lowered himself. When the horse stopped rearing in protest against the weight on its back, the trainer mounted. Patting the animal's neck, he urged the horse to move by digging his heels into its sides. While the halter might have to be jerked several times to obtain obedience, there was rarely any bucking and most horses quickly learned to respond to the rider's commands.

Other tribes used a more direct method to break a horse. The animal was lassoed—one lariat being thrown over the neck and kept taut, making breathing difficult—and thrown to the ground, where it was hobbled in such a way that every time it tried to stand it would fall down. Only when the horse was completely exhausted from its struggles was it mounted. Osage trainers employed a far gentler technique. They tied a wild horse to a broken one for a week. This usually made the animal docile enough to accept a rider.

A man's pad saddle, Blackfoot

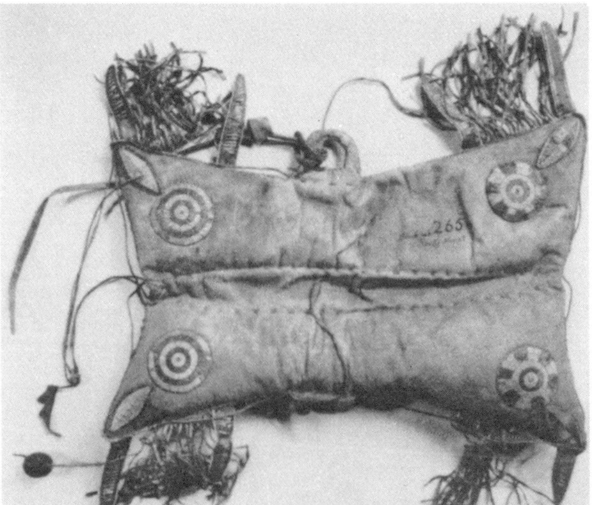

Two Indian "ponies" dominate Kurz drawing of Young Elk, chief of the Omaha. Note bells on mount, and pictograph on clothing of chief.

To an Indian, a horse's appearance was almost as important as its speed and endurance. Plains Indians made their mounts more attractive by plaiting bright ribbons into their tails and manes and hanging strings of tiny bells or bear claw necklaces on their necks. When Lieutenant Lawrence Kip of the United States Cavalry scouted the Walla Walla in 1855, he reported that their horses ". . . had beads and fringes of gaudy colors hanging from their bridles, while the plumes of eagle feathers interwoven with the mane and tail, fluttered as the breeze swept over them, and completed their wild and fantastic appearance."

While no tribe docked tails—a cruel practice which "civilized" peoples believed improved their horses' looks—the red

Indians preparing to attend a festive occasion. The horse too is wearing elaborate beadwork on bridle and saddle blanket. Note the inset from the man's jacket, showing a mounted Indian "casting a cord." From the photo archive of St. Francis Indian Mission to the Rosebud Sioux, St. Francis, South Dakota; photo by Reverend Eugene Buechel, S.J.

The Great White Stallion gallops through the legends of all horse-owning tribes.

man did slit or trim the ears of his favorite mount. While this mutilation supposedly improved the animal's looks, it also had a practical value—it enabled warriors to identify a horse in the dark.

Because the Plains Indians delighted in spotted and mottled horses—which were not only attractive but also blended into the landscape—solid-colored animals were frequently painted in contrasting shades. Braves would smear white horses with red and brown dyes made from plants or roots and plaster dark horses with white clay.

Pintos—the name comes from the Spanish *pintado*, meaning painted or spotted—were the Plains Indians' favorite mounts. According to the Comanche, all Pintos were descendants of the Great White Stallion which gallops through the legends of all horse-owning tribes. Actually, the origin of the Pinto is a mystery.

The Pinto of the Indians with its "hang-dog expression so little suggestive of its exhaustive stamina" bears little resemblance to the Pintos exhibited at modern horse shows. Nevertheless, "Old Paint" is as much a symbol of the West of yesteryear as is the buffalo.

While the average Indian "pony" had tremendous stamina, its only attractive feature was its mottled hide. Either brown and white or black and white, it was a small, narrow-chested animal which usually had "one wicked glass eye that showed the latent devil in his heart." But there were many exceptions to this generalization. Certain mustangs displayed the qualities inherited from the "selected stock" shipped to New Spain. Then, too, a number of tribes engaged in selective breeding of horses, and their herds were composed of outstanding animals. The

The Pinto, beloved of the Plains tribes. The mare pictured here is a registered Half-Arabian which was bred to the purebred Arabian stallion Gawad (opposite). *The resulting colt is a three-quarters Arabian Pinto.*

R.V.'s Pat Domino, registered Appaloosa stallion, descendant of the horses bred by the Nez Percé Indians.

most successful of all Indian horse breeders were the Nez Percé.

When Lewis and Clark visited the Nez Percé in 1806, they reported, "Their horses appear to be of an excellent race. They are . . . elegantly formed, active and durable. . . . Some of these horses are pided with large spots of white irregularly scattered and intermixed with black, brown, bay or some other dark color."

These beautiful animals had been developed by the Nez Percé from spotted horses they had acquired in trade from Mexico in the early seventeenth century. The breed, known as the Appaloosa—a name derived from the region where it originated—is the first multi-colored horse to be successfully bred in North America.

Appaloosas come in many colors, but they all have certain characteristics.

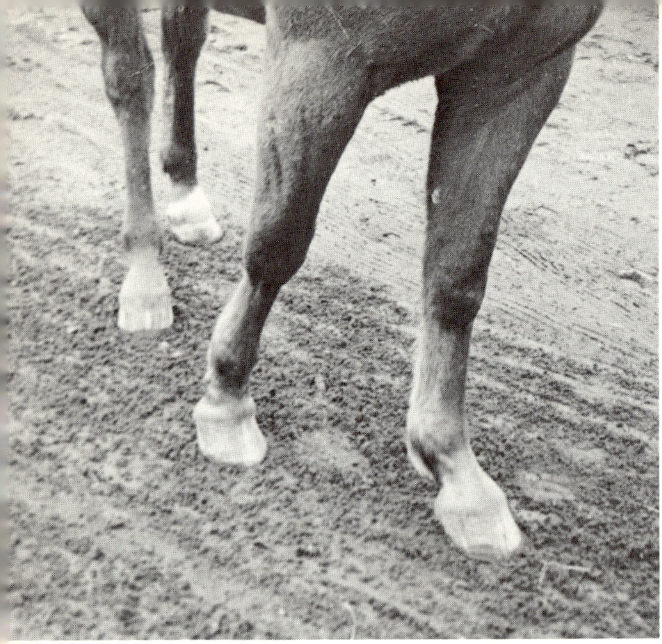

Appaloosa characteristics: black and white vertical stripes on hoofs (note rear right hoof particularly);

"If horses were dogs, the Appaloosa would be a Dalmation." However, while the majority of Appaloosas are white with dark spots on the hips and around the head (the latter blend and give the effect of a solid color), many of the breed are dark blue, brown, gray, or roan with white spots. Some Appaloosas also have vertical stripes of black and white on their hoofs.

sclera, or white surrounding eye;

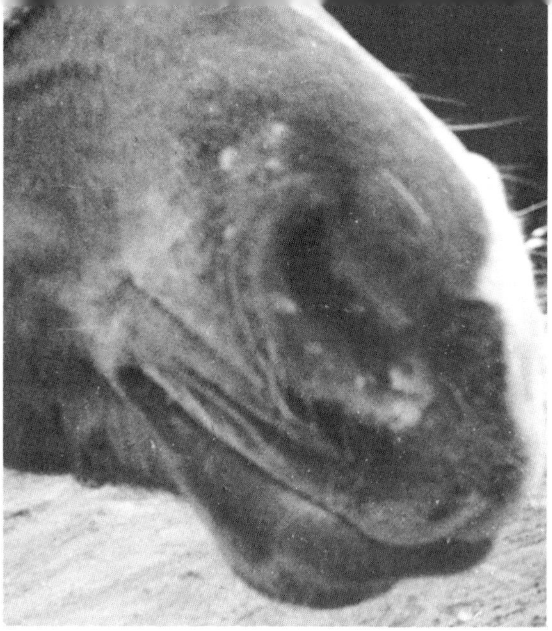

mottling and whiskers around nose;

spots—some have more than others—and a broom tail.

There was just as much variation in the quality of the Appaloosas bred by the Nez Percé as in their coloring. Therefore, the Nez Percé divided their horses into four groups. The first consisted of inferior specimens which were traded to other tribes. They used animals of a slightly better grade as pack horses and as mounts for the elderly. Animals of still better quality were employed for routine riding by the men of the tribe. Very fast and exceptionally attractive horses were trained as buffalo runners and war horses.

Along with selecting breeding stock carefully, the Nez Percé engaged in superstitious rites to insure that foals would have the characteristic Appaloosa mottling. Pregnant mares were daubed with a paint compounded by a secret formula. This paint was also applied to the mare's hips with the thumb and fingers extended as far apart as possible. This, the Nez Percé believed, would cause a foal to be spotted.

In 1877, the Great White Father broke his treaty with the Nez Percé and Chief Joseph led the tribe northward. In the battles that took place during this 1600-mile journey, three thousand Appaloosas were killed and, when the Nez Percé were finally defeated, they turned the remainder of their horses loose. Nor did the few tribesmen who had refused to follow Chief Joseph retain their mounts. They were forced to give them up by missionaries who reasoned that if the Nez Percé lacked horses they would stop wandering and become farmers.

Although the herds of the Nez Percé were scattered throughout the Plains, the Appaloosa did not disappear. Its spirit, stamina, and striking appearance attracted the attention of horsemen who not only kept the breed alive but also improved its quality. Today, registered Appaloosas are ridden in show and rodeo competition and used for stock handling. There is little doubt that Chief Joseph himself would approve of their bearing, coloring, and performance.

With the vanishing of the buffalo herds and the confinement of the Plains Indians to reservations, the quality of the red man's mounts declined. Forced to follow the white man's road instead of being free to gallop in all directions, the prairie dwellers stopped capturing mustangs. But while the Plains Indians no longer had any need of buffalo runners or war horses, they continued to take pride in their mounts. They still do. A number of tribes are actively engaged in the selective breeding

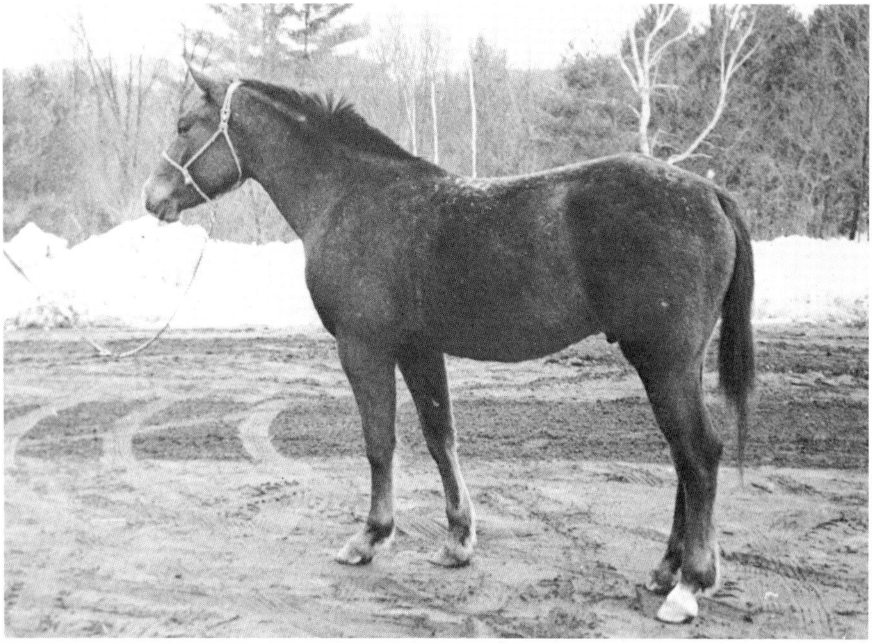

Some Appaloosas are more flashy than others but both of these show blanket of spots.

The Navajo and his horses today, at the annual Intertribal Indian Ceremonials at Gallup, New Mexico, in August.

of horses, using both the age-old techniques of their ancestors and modern methods to improve their stock.

Even as the Horse Culture Period was drawing to a close, some homesteaders were relying on "stallion steak and mare stew" to keep their families alive whenever crops failed. But the white settlers soon learned that wild horses not only lured domestic stock to freedom but also that mustangs ate the grass needed by cattle. As a result, a wholesale slaughtering of wild horses was inaugurated. Thousands upon thousands were driven over cliffs in California to drown in the Pacific Ocean, while owners of large "spreads" exterminated the mustangs on their property by hiring professional horse hunters. In more recent years, "sportsmen" have shot many wild horses and modern mustangers have rounded up thousands and sold them to makers of glue and dog food.

Navajo night riders sing the "Fire Dance Chant" at the night show.

After the Ceremonials are over, the horses pull the family wagon back toward the vast Navajo Reservation.

Thanks to the efforts of conservationists, wild horses run free today in the Pryor Mountains of Montana.

Only the efforts of conservationists and horse lovers have kept the mustang from becoming extinct. Some individuals have spent years searching for outstanding stallions and mares among surviving bands in order to breed them. Meanwhile, in isolated regions of nine western states, small bands of wild horses graze in refuges.

But even this minute fraction of the tremendous number of wild horses that once darkened the Plains could vanish. This is because all mustangs are classified as feral and, generally speaking, domesticated animals that have gone wild are not covered by the laws that protect game. Therefore, further legislation must be enacted to save the few remaining bands of wild horses.

The International Society for the Protection of Mustangs and Burros and other organizations are actively engaged in a campaign to secure additional ranges for wild horses on public lands. It is to be hoped that they succeed. Otherwise, the thunder created by the hoofs of the horses the Indians rode will no longer echo from canyon rimrock and mountainside.

Index

SIGMUND A. LAVINE was highly active while in college; he wrote features for the *Boston Sunday Post* and covered Boston University sports for two wire services. After receiving his M.A., he taught in a United States Government Indian School at Belcourt, North Dakota, for two years, learned to speak both the Sioux and Cree languages and talk in sign language. He was invited to tribal dances, ceremonies, and Indian Court in reservations throughout Canada and the Northwest.

Sigmund Lavine has taught in the Boston schools for over thirty years and is now an assistant principal. He also lectures and writes literary criticism.

With his wife—and a whippet answering to the unlikely name of Morrisey, the latest in a long line of prize-winning dogs owned by the Lavines—he lives in a house filled with books, fish tanks, historical china, art glass, and the largest privately owned collection of Gilbert and Sullivan material in America. For relaxation the Lavines attend country auctions, go "antiquing," or browse in bookstores, but their greatest pleasure is truck gardening on a piece of rocky New Hampshire land.